More to be Desired than Gold

What Jesus said about the Word in the Gospels

JoAnn Jernigan

ISBN 978-1-64258-821-7 (paperback)
ISBN 978-1-64258-823-1 (hardcover)
ISBN 978-1-64258-822-4 (digital)

Christian Faith Publishing, Inc.
832 Park Avenue
Meadville, PA 16335
www.christianfaithpublishing.com

Printed in the United States of America

The Word of God is

The Law of the LORD *is* perfect, converting the soul;
The Testimony of the LORD *is* sure, making wise the simple;
The Statutes of the LORD *are* right, rejoicing the heart;
The Commandment of the LORD *is* pure, enlightening the eyes;
The fear of the LORD *is* clean, enduring forever;
The Judgments of the LORD *are* true *and* righteous altogether.

More to be desired *are they* than gold,
Yea, than much fine gold;
Sweeter also than honey and the honeycomb.
Moreover by them Your servant is warned,
And in keeping them *there is* great reward.

Psalm 19:7-11

Table of Contents

Matthew 4:4

But He (Jesus) answered and said, *"It is written,* 'Man shall not live by bread alone, but by every word that proceeds from the mouth of God.'"

Matthew 4:7

Jesus said to him, *"It is written* again, 'You shall not tempt the LORD your God.'"

Matthew 4:10

Then Jesus said to him, "Away with you, Satan! For *it is written*, 'You shall worship the LORD your God, and Him only you shall serve.'"

Matthew 5:17–18

"Do not think that I came to destroy *the law or the prophets*. I did not come to destroy but to fulfill.

[18] For assuredly, I say to you, till heaven and earth pass away, one jot or one tittle will by no means pass from the law till all is fulfilled.

It Is Written,

Man shall not *Live* by *Bread Alone,* but by EVERY WORD THAT PROCEEDS FROM THE Mouth of GOD, DO NOT THINK that I came to **Destroy the Law** OR THE PROPHETS. I DID NOT come to DESTROY but to **FULFILL.**

For assuredly, I say to you, till Heaven and Earth pass away, one jot or one tittle will *BY NO MEANS* pass from the Law till ALL IS FULFILLED.

Matthew 5:19

Whoever therefore breaks one of the least of *these commandments*, **and teaches men so, shall be called least in the kingdom of heaven; but whoever does and teaches** *them*, **he shall be called great in the kingdom of heaven.**

Matthew 5:21–22

"You have heard that it was said to those of old, 'You shall not murder and whoever murders will be in danger of the judgment.' [22] But I say to you that whoever is angry with his brother without a cause shall be in danger of the judgment. And whoever says to his brother, 'Raca!' shall be in danger of the council. But whoever says, 'You fool!' shall be in danger of hell fire.
(Refers to Ex. 20:13, Deut. 5:17)

Matthew 5:27–28

"You have heard that it was said to those of old, 'You shall not commit adultery.' [28] **But I say to you that whoever looks at a woman to lust for her has already committed adultery with her in his heart."**
(Refers to Ex. 20:14, Deut. 5:18)

Whoever therefore BREAKS one of the LEAST of these Commandments, & TEACHES MEN SO, SHALL BE CALLED LEAST in the Kingdom of Heaven; BUT whoever DOES & TEACHES THEM, HE SHALL BE CALLED GREAT in the Kingdom of Heaven.

You have heard that it was said to those of old, 'You shall not commit Adultery.' BUT I SAY TO YOU THAT WHOEVER LOOKS AT A WOMAN TO LUST FOR HER HAS ALREADY COMMITTED ADULTERY WITH HER IN HIS HEART.

Matthew 5:38–39

"You have heard that it was said, 'An eye for an eye and a tooth for a tooth.'

[39] **But I tell you** not to resist an evil person. But **whoever slaps you on your right cheek, turn the other to him also.**"

Matthew 5:43–44

"You have heard that it was said, 'You shall love your neighbor and hate your enemy.' [44] **But I say to you, love your enemies, bless those who curse you, do good to those who hate you, and pray for those who spitefully use you and persecute you...**"
(Refers to Lev. 19:18)

Matthew 7:12

Therefore, whatever you want men to do to you, do also to them, for this is the Law and the Prophets.

Matthew 7:21–23

"Not everyone who says to Me, 'Lord, Lord,' shall enter the kingdom of heaven, but he who does *the will of My Father* in heaven. [22] Many will say to Me in that day, 'Lord, Lord, have we not prophesied in Your name, cast out demons in Your name, and done many wonders in Your name?' [23] And then I will declare to them, 'I never knew you; depart from Me, you who practice *lawlessness!*'

You have heard that it was said,

'An eye for an eye and a tooth for a tooth.'

BUT I TELL YOU...

WHOEVER SLAPS YOU ON YOUR RIGHT CHEEK,

TURN THE OTHER TO HIM ALSO.

You have heard that it was said, 'You shall love your neighbor and hate your enemy.'

BUT I SAY TO YOU,

LOVE YOUR ENEMIES,

BLESS THOSE WHO CURSE YOU,

DO GOOD TO THOSE WHO HATE YOU,

AND PRAY FOR THOSE WHO SPITEFULLY USE YOU AND PERSECUTE YOU,....

Not Everyone who says to Me,

'Lord, Lord,'

SHALL ENTER THE KINGDOM OF HEAVEN,

but HE WHO

Does The Will

OF MY FATHER IN HEAVEN.

Matthew 7:24–27

"Therefore whoever hears these sayings of Mine, and does them, I will liken him to a wise man who built his house on the rock

²⁵ and **the rain descended, the floods came, and the winds blew** and beat on that house; **and it did not fall, for it was founded on the rock.**

²⁶ **"But everyone who hears** *these sayings of Mine*, **and does not do them, will be like a foolish man who built his house on the sand:** ²⁷ and the rain descended, the floods came, and the winds blew and beat on that house; and it fell. **And great was its fall."**

Matthew 9:11–13

¹¹ And when the Pharisees saw *it*, they said to His disciples, "Why does your Teacher eat with tax collectors and sinners?" ¹² When Jesus heard *that*, He said to them, "Those who are well have no need of a physician, but those who are sick. ¹³ But go and learn what *this* means: 'I desire mercy and not sacrifice.' For I did not come to call the righteous, but sinners, to repentance. (Refers to Hos. 6:6)

Matthew 11:10

For this is *he* of whom *it is written*: 'Behold, I send My messenger** before your face, who will prepare your way before You. (Refers to Mal. 3:1)

Therefore whoever hears these sayings of Mine,

and DOES THEM,

I will liken him to a WISE man

who built his house on the **Rock** ...

The Rain descended,

The Floods came,

And the Winds blew...

and it did NOT FALL for it was

FOUNDED on the **ROCK.**

But Everyone who Hears

these Sayings of Mine, &

DOES **NOT** DO THEM,

will be like a FOOLISH man

who built his house on the Sand..:

And great was its FALL!

For this is he of whom IT IS WRITTEN:

Behold, I send My messenger... *John*

Matthew 12:1-8

At that time Jesus went through the grainfields on the Sabbath. And His disciples were hungry, and began to pluck heads of grain and to eat.
2 **And when the Pharisees saw** *it***, they said to Him, "Look, Your disciples are doing what is** *not lawful* **to do on the Sabbath!"**

3 **But He said to them, "Have you not read what David did when he was hungry, he and those who were with him:** 4 **how he entered the house of God and ate the showbread which was not** *lawful* **for him to eat,** nor for those who were with him, but only for the priests?

5 **Or** *have you not read* **in the law that on the Sabbath the priests in the temple profane the Sabbath, and are blameless?** 6 **Yet I say to you that in this place there is One greater than the temple.**

7 **But if you had known what this means, 'I desire mercy and not sacrifice,'** **you would not have condemned the guiltless.** (Refers to Hos. 6:6)
8 **For the Son of Man is Lord even of the Sabbath."**

And when the Pharisees saw *it*, they said to Him, "Look, Your disciples are doing *what is not lawful* to do on the Sabbath!"

But He said to them, "*Have you not read* what David did when he was hungry, he and those who were with him: how he entered the House of God and ate the showbread which was *not lawful* for him to eat...

Or *have you not read in the Law* that on the Sabbath the priests in the temple profane the Sabbath, and are blameless?

Yet I say to you that in this place there is **One Greater** than the Temple.

But if you had known what this means,

'*I desire Mercy & not Sacrifice,*'

you would not have CONDEMNED the GUILTLESS.

for THE SON OF MAN IS *Lord* EVEN OF THE *Sabbath.*"

Matthew 12:38-42

Then some of the scribes and Pharisees answered, saying, "Teacher, we want to see a sign from You."

[39] But He answered and said to them,

"**An evil and adulterous generation seeks after a sign, and no sign will be given to it except the sign of the prophet Jonah.**

[40] **For as Jonah was three days and three nights in the belly of the great fish, so will the Son of Man be three days and three nights in the heart of the earth.**
(Refers to Jonah 1:17)

[41] The men of Nineveh will rise up in the judgment with this generation and condemn it,

because they repented at the preaching of Jonah; and **indeed a greater than Jonah is here.**
(Refers to Jer. 3:11, Jonah 3:5)

[42] The queen of the South will rise up in the judgment with this generation and condemn it, for she came from the ends of the earth to hear the wisdom of Solomon; and indeed a greater than Solomon is here.
(Refers to I Kings 10: 1-13)

An Evil and Adulterous Generation

SEEKS AFTER A **SIGN,**

& NO SIGN WILL BE GIVEN TO IT

Except

the sign of the Prophet Jonah.

For as **Jonah** was

3 Days & **3 Nights**

IN THE BELLY OF THE GREAT FISH,

so will the **Son of Man** *be*

3 Days & **3 Nights**

IN THE HEART OF THE EARTH.

…INDEED **A Greater**

than Jonah

is HERE.

Matthew 13:14–18

And in them the prophecy of *Isaiah is fulfilled*, which says: 'Hearing you will hear and shall not understand and seeing you will see and not perceive;

[15] **For the hearts of this people have grown dull.** *Their* **ears are hard of hearing, and their eyes they have closed, lest they should see with** *their* **eyes and hear with** *their* **ears, Lest they should understand with their hearts and turn, so that I should heal them.'**

[16] **But blessed are your eyes for they see, and your ears for they hear;**

[17] for assuredly, I say to you that many prophets and righteous *men* desired to see what you see, and did not see *it*, and to hear what you hear, and did not hear *it*.

[18] **Therefore, hear the parable of the sower:**
(Refers to Is. 6:9-10)

And in them (the parables) the **Prophecy of Isaiah** *is fulfilled*, which says:

'Hearing you will Hear

and shall **NOT** Understand

and seeing you will See

and **NOT** Perceive;

for the hearts of this people have grown **DULL.**

Their Ears are Hard of Hearing,

and their Eyes they have Closed,

lest they should See with their Eyes

and Hear with their Ears,

lest they should understand with their Hearts

and **TURN, so that I should HEAL them.'**

But Blessed are your Eyes

for they SEE,

and your Ears

for they HEAR...

Therefore, Hear the parable of the Sower.

Matthew 13: 19–23

When anyone hears the word of the kingdom, and does not understand it, then the wicked *one* comes and snatches away what was sown in his heart. This is he who received seed by the wayside.

[20] But he who received the seed on stony places, this is he who hears the word and immediately receives it with joy;

[21] yet he has no root in himself, but endures only for a while. For when tribulation or persecution arises because of the word, immediately he stumbles.

[22] Now he who received seed among the thorns is he who hears the word, and **the cares of this world and the deceitfulness of riches choke the word**, and he becomes unfruitful.

[23] But **he who received seed on the good ground is he who hears the word and understands** *it*, who indeed **bears fruit and produces: some a hundredfold, some sixty, some thirty.**"

Matthew 13:34–35

All these things Jesus spoke to the multitude in parables; and without a parable He did not speak to them,

[35] that it might be fulfilled which was spoken by the prophet, saying: "I will open My mouth in parables; I will utter things kept secret from the foundation of the world."
(Refers to Ps. 78:2)

When anyone HEARS
the Word of the Kingdom,
and DOES NOT UNDERSTAND it,

THEN *the* **wicked one** *comes*

& snatches away

what was Sown in his Heart.

...the cares of this world &

the deceitfulness of riches

CHOKE THE WORD ...

But he who received

Seed on the good ground

is he who HEARS the Word & UNDERSTANDS It.

who indeed BEARS FRUIT & PRODUCES:

some a 100X, some 60, some 30.

Matthew 15:3–9

He answered and said to them, **"Why do you also transgress *the commandment of God* because of your tradition?** [4] For *God commanded*, saying, 'Honor your father and your mother'; and, 'He who curses father or mother, let him be put to death.' [5] But you say, 'Whoever says to his father or mother, "Whatever profit you might have received from me *is* a gift to God"— [6] then he need not honor his father or mother.' **Thus you have made *the commandment of God* of no effect by your tradition.** [7] **Hypocrites!** Well did Isaiah prophesy about you, saying: [8] 'These people draw near to Me with their mouth, and honor Me with *their* lips, but **their heart is far from Me**. [9] **And in vain they worship Me, teaching as doctrines the commandments of men.'"** (Refers to Ex. 20:12, 21:17; Deut. 5:16; Is. 29:13)

Matthew 16:4

A wicked and adulterous generation seeks after a sign, and no sign shall be given to it except the sign of the prophet Jonah. (Refers to the O.T. book of Jonah)

WHY DO YOU ALSO *TRANSGRESS*

The Commandment of God

BECAUSE OF YOUR

Tradition?!!

THUS you have made

The Commandment of God

OF NO EFFECT

BY your Tradition!

HYPOCRITES!

...their Heart is far from Me.

And IN VAIN

they worship Me,

TEACHING AS DOCTRINES

the commandments of MEN.

Matthew 18:16

But if he will not hear, take with you one or two more, that **'by the mouth of two or three witnesses every word may be established.'**
(Refers to Duet. 19:15)

Matthew 19:3–5, 8

The Pharisees also came to Him, testing Him, and saying to Him, "Is it lawful for a man to divorce his wife for *just* any reason?"

[4] And He answered and said to them, "Have you not read that He who made *them* at the beginning 'made them male and female,'
[5] and said, **'For this reason a man shall leave his father and mother and be joined to his wife, and the two shall become one flesh'?**
[8] He said to them, **"Moses, because of the hardness of your hearts, permitted you to divorce your wives, but from the beginning it was not so.**
(Refers to Gen. 1:27, 5:2, 2:24)

Matthew 19:17–19

So He said to him, **"Why do you call Me good? No one *is* good but One, *that is*, God. But if you want to enter into life, keep the commandments."**

[18] He said to Him, "Which ones?" Jesus said, "'You shall not murder,' 'You shall not commit adultery,' 'You shall not steal,' 'You shall not bear false witness,'
[19] 'Honor your father and *your* mother,' and, 'You shall love your neighbor as yourself.'"

...'by the mouth of two or three witnesses Every Word may be Established.'

And He answered and said to them, "HAVE YOU NOT READ THAT He who made them At the Beginning 'made them Male and Female...' 'FOR THIS REASON a man shall LEAVE HIS FATHER AND MOTHER and be joined to his wife, and the TWO SHALL BECOME ONE FLESH'?

...Moses, because of the HARDNESS of your hearts, permitted you to divorce your wives, but from the Beginning it was NOT SO...

But if you want to enter into Life, KEEP the Commandments."

16

Matthew 21:13–16

And He said to them, *"It is written*, 'My house shall be called a house of prayer,' but you have made it a 'den of thieves.'"
[14] Then the blind and the lame came to Him in the temple, and He healed them.
[15] But when the chief priests and scribes saw the wonderful things that He did, and the children crying out in the temple and saying, "Hosanna to the Son of David!" they were indignant
[16] and said to Him, "Do You hear what these are saying?" And Jesus said to them, "Yes. **Have you never read, 'Out of the mouth of babes and nursing infants you have perfected praise'?"**
(Refers to Is. 56:7, Jer. 7:11, Ps. 8:2)

Matthew 21:42–43

Jesus said to them, "Have you never read in *the Scriptures*: 'The stone which the builders rejected has become the chief cornerstone. This was the LORD's doing, and it is marvelous in our eyes'?"
[43] "Therefore I say to you, the kingdom of God will be taken from you and given to a nation bearing the fruits of it. (Refers to Ps.118:22-23)

And He said to them, "IT IS WRITTEN,

'My House shall be called A House of Prayer,'

but you have made it

a 'DEN of THEIVES.'"

"Have you never read, 'Out of the mouth of babes and nursing infants you have PERFECTED PRAISE'?"

Jesus said to them,

"Have you never read in the Scriptures:

'THE STONE

WHICH THE BUILDERS

REJECTED

HAS BECOME THE

CHIEF CORNER STONE.

THIS WAS THE LORD'S DOING,

and it is Marvelous in our eyes'?"

17

Matthew 22:29–32

Jesus answered and said to them, "You are mistaken, not knowing *the Scriptures* nor the power of God.
[30] For in the resurrection they neither marry nor are given in marriage, but are like angels of God in heaven.
[31] But concerning the resurrection of the dead, *have you not read* what was *spoken to you by God, saying,*
[32] 'I am the God of Abraham, the God of Isaac, and the God of Jacob'? God is not the God of the dead, but of the living."
(Refers to Ex. 3:6, 15)

Matthew 22:36–40

"Teacher, which *is* the great *commandment in the law?"*
[37] Jesus said to him, "You shall love the Lord your God with all your heart, with all your soul, and with all your mind.
[38] This is *the first and great commandment.*
[39] And *the* second *is* like it: You shall love your neighbor as yourself.
[40] On these two commandments hang all the law and the prophets."
(Refers to Deut. 6:5, Lev. 19:18)

Jesus answered and said to them,

"You are mistaken,

not knowing the Scriptures

NOR THE POWER OF GOD.

...have you not READ what was

SPOKEN TO YOU BY GOD,

saying, 'I am the God of Abraham, the God of Isaac, and the God of Jacob'?

God isn't the God of the Dead, but of the Living."

"TEACHER, WHICH IS THE GREAT COMMANDMENT IN THE LAW?" JESUS SAID TO HIM,

"You shall LOVE the Lord your God

with ALL your heart,

with ALL your soul,

and with ALL your mind.

THIS IS THE 1ST & GREAT COMMANDMENT.

AND THE 2ND IS LIKE IT:

You shall LOVE your Neighbor as Yourself.

ON THESE TWO COMMANDMENTS

HANG ALL THE LAW & THE PROPHETS."

Matthew 22:41–46

While the Pharisees were gathered together, Jesus asked them, [42] **saying, "What do you think about the Christ? Whose Son is He?" They said to Him, "*The Son* of David."** [43] He said to them, "How then does David in the Spirit call Him 'Lord,' saying: [44] 'The LORD said to my Lord, "Sit at My right hand, till I make Your enemies Your footstool"'? [45] **If David then calls Him 'Lord,' how is He his Son?"** [46] And no one was able to answer Him a word, nor from that day on did anyone dare question Him anymore. (Refers to Ps. 110:1)

Matthew 23:23–24

"Woe to you, scribes and Pharisees, hypocrites! For you pay tithe of mint and anise and cumin, and **have neglected the weightier matters of the law: justice and mercy and faith. These you ought to have done, without leaving the others undone.** [24] **Blind guides, who strain out a gnat and swallow a camel!**

While the Pharisees

were gathered together,

Jesus asked them, saying,

"What do you think about the Christ?

Whose Son is He?"

They said to Him, "*The Son* of David."

"If David then

calls Him 'Lord',

how is He his Son?"

WOE TO YOU,

scribes & Pharisees, hypocrites!

For you... have NEGLECTED the Weightier Matters of the Law:

JUSTICE

& MERCY

& FAITH.

These you ought to have done, without leaving the others undone.

BLIND GUIDES,

who strain out a gnat

& swallow a camel !

Matthew 24:8-16, 37-39

"All these *are* the beginning of sorrows.
⁹ Then they will deliver you up to tribulation and kill you, and you will be hated by all nations for My name's sake.

¹⁰ **And then many will be offended, will betray one another, and will hate one another.**

¹¹ Then **many false prophets** will rise up and deceive many.
¹² And because *lawlessness* will abound, *the love of many will grow cold.*

¹³ **But he who endures to the end shall be saved.**
¹⁴ **And this** *gospel of the kingdom* **will be preached in all the world as a witness to all the nations, and then the end will come."**

¹⁵ "Therefore when you see the 'abomination of desolation,' spoken of by Daniel the prophet, standing in the holy place" (whoever reads, let him understand),
¹⁶ "then let those who are in Judea flee to the mountains.
(Refers to Dan. 11:31, 12:11)

³⁷ But as the days of Noah were, so also will the coming of the Son of Man be.
³⁸ For as in the days before the flood, they were eating and drinking, marrying and giving in marriage, until the day that Noah entered the ark,
³⁹ and did not know until the flood came and took them all away, so also will the coming of the Son of Man be.

All these are the
Beginning of Sorrows.
And then many will be offended,
will betray one another,
and will hate one another.
Many False Prophets...
Lawlessness will abound,
The LOVE of many GROW COLD.
But he who Endures TO THE END
Shall BE SAVED.

And This Gospel of the Kingdom
will be preached
in All the World
as a witness
to ALL the nations, &
then THE END will come.

Matthew 26:24, 31

(Jesus said) **"The Son of Man indeed *goes just as it is written* of Him, but woe to that man by whom the Son of Man is betrayed!** It would have been good for that man if he had not been born."
[31] Then Jesus said to them, **"All of you will be made to stumble because of Me this night, for *it is written*: 'I will strike the Shepherd, and the sheep of the flock will be scattered.'** (Refers to Zech. 13:7)

Matthew 26:53–56

Or do you think that I cannot now pray to My Father, and He will provide Me with more than twelve legions of angels?
[54] How then could the *Scriptures* be fulfilled, that it must happen thus?"
[55] **In that hour Jesus said to the multitudes, "Have you come out, as against a robber, with swords and clubs to take Me?** I sat daily with you, teaching in the temple, and you did not seize Me.
[56] **But all this was done that the *Scriptures of the prophets* might be fulfilled."** Then all the disciples forsook Him and fled.

The Son of Man INDEED GOES JUST AS IT IS *Written of Him,* BUT WOE TO THAT MAN BY WHOM THE SON OF MAN *is* BETRAYED! *All of you will be made to Stumble because of Me this night, for It Is Written:* 'I WILL *STRIKE THE SHEPHERD,* & THE SHEEP OF THE FLOCK WILL BE SCATTERED.' *In that hour Jesus said to the multitudes,* "Have you come out, as against a robber, with swords and clubs to take Me?" *"But all this was done that The Scriptures of the prophets Might Be Fulfilled."* Then all the disciples FORSOOK HIM & FLED.

Matthew 27:46

And about the ninth hour Jesus cried out with a loud voice, saying, "Eli, Eli, lama sabachthani?" that is, **"My God, My God, why have You forsaken Me?"**
(Refers to Ps. 22:1)

Matthew 28:19–20

Go therefore and make disciples of all the nations, baptizing them in the name of the Father and of the Son and of the Holy Spirit,

[20] **teaching them to observe all things that** *I have commanded you;* **and lo, I am with you always, even to the end of the age."**
Amen.

And about the 9th hour Jesus cried out. . . ,

"My God, My God,

why have You Forsaken Me?"

GO therefore

& Make Disciples

of ALL the NATIONS,

Baptizing them in the

Name of The Father

and of The Son

and of The Holy Spirit,

Teaching them to OBSERVE ALL THINGS

that I have Commanded YOU;

And Lo, I AM with you Always,

even to **the END of the AGE.** *Amen.*

Mark

Mark 1:15
(Jesus) . . . saying, **"The time is fulfilled, and the kingdom of God is at hand. Repent, and believe in *the gospel*."**

Mark 1:44
(Jesus) . . . said to him, "See that you say nothing to anyone; but go your way, show yourself to the priest, and offer for your cleansing those things which *Moses commanded*, as a testimony to them."

Mark 2:25–28
But He said to them, **"Have you *never read* what David did** when he was in need and hungry, he and those with him:
[26] how he went into the house of God *in the days* of Abiathar the high priest, and ate the showbread, which is not lawful to eat except for the priests, and also gave some to those who were with him?"
[27] And He said to them, **"The Sabbath was made for man, and not man for the Sabbath.**
[28] Therefore **the Son of Man is also Lord of the Sabbath."**

Mark 3:4-5
Then He said to them, ***"Is it lawful** on the Sabbath to do good or to do evil, to save life or to kill?"* But they kept silent.
[5] And when He had looked around at them with anger, being grieved by the hardness of their hearts, He said to the man, "Stretch out your hand." And he stretched it out, and **his hand was restored as whole as the other.**

"THE Time IS FULFILLED, &

The Kingdom of God is AT HAND.

REPENT, &

BELIEVE in the Gospel."

"Have you never read what David did…?"

"The Sabbath

WAS MADE FOR MAN,

and NOT man for the Sabbath.

…the Son of Man is also

Lord of the Sabbath."

"Is it Lawful on the Sabbath

to DO GOOD or to DO EVIL,

to save life or to kill?"

…his hand was RESTORED

as WHOLE as the other.

Mark 4:10-12

But when He was alone, those around Him with the twelve asked Him about the parable. [11] And He said to them, "To you it has been given to know the mystery of the kingdom of God; but to those who are outside, all things come in parables, [12] so that 'Seeing they may see and not perceive, and hearing they may hear and not understand; Lest they should turn, and their sins be forgiven them.'
(Refers to Is. 6:9-10)

Mark 4:14–19

The sower sows *the word*. [15] And these are the ones by the wayside where *the word* is sown. When they hear, Satan comes immediately and takes away *the word* that was sown in their hearts. [16] These likewise are the ones sown on stony ground who, when they hear *the word*, immediately receive it with gladness; [17] and they have no root in themselves, and so endure only for a time. Afterward, when tribulation or persecution arises for *the word's* sake, immediately they stumble. [18] Now these are the ones sown among thorns; *they are* the ones who hear the word, [19] and the cares of this world, the deceitfulness of riches, and the desires for other things entering in choke *the word*, and it becomes unfruitful.

THE SOWER *Sows* THE WORD.

And these are the ones

by the Wayside

where the Word is sown.

WHEN THEY HEAR,

Satan comes *immediately* & TAKES AWAY

THE WORD … sown in their hearts.

Afterward,

When TRIBULATION OR PERSECUTION

Arises for the Word's sake,

Immediately THEY STUMBLE.

…the Cares of this World,

the Deceitfulness of Riches,

& the Desires for other things

ENTERING IN

Choke the Word,

and it becomes Unfruitful.

Mark 4:20

But these are the ones sown on good ground, those who hear the word, accept it, and bear fruit: some thirtyfold, some sixty, and some a hundred.

Mark 7:6–10

He answered and said to them, "Well did Isaiah prophesy of you hypocrites, as it is written: 'This people honors Me with their lips, but their heart is far from Me. [7] And **in vain they worship Me, teaching *as doctrines* the commandments of men**. [8] For laying aside *the commandment* of God, you hold the tradition of men— the washing of pitchers and cups, and many other such things you do." [9] He said to them, ***"All too* well you reject *the commandment* of God, that you may keep your tradition.** [10] For Moses said, 'Honor your father and your mother'; and, 'He who curses father or mother, let him be put to death.'

Mark 7:13

. . . making *the word of God* **of no effect through your tradition** which you have handed down. And many such things you do.

But these are the ones

SOWN on good ground,

those who HEAR THE WORD,

ACCEPT IT, and bear fruit...

IN VAIN *they Worship Me,*

TEACHING AS DOCTRINES

the COMMANDMENTS

of Men.

All too well

you reject

the Commandment of God,

THAT YOU MAY KEEP YOUR TRADITION.

...making the Word of God

OF NO EFFECT

through your **Tradition...**

Mark 8:35

For whoever desires to save his life will lose it, but whoever loses his life for My sake and *the gospel's* will save it.

Mark 8:38

For whoever is ashamed of Me and *My words* in this adulterous and sinful generation, of him the Son of Man also will be ashamed when He comes in the glory of His Father with the holy angels.

Mark 9:12–13

Then He answered and told them, "Indeed, Elijah is coming first and restores all things. And how *is it written* concerning the Son of Man, that He must suffer many things and be treated with contempt?

[13] But I say to you that Elijah has also come, and they did to him whatever they wished, as *it is written* of him."

For whoever desires
to SAVE his life
WILL LOSE IT,
But whoever LOSES his life
for MY SAKE
and the GOSPEL'S
WILL SAVE IT.
For whoever is Ashamed
OF ME & MY WORDS
in this Adulterous &
Sinful Generation,
OF HIM
The Son of Man
also will be Ashamed
when He comes in the
GLORY OF HIS FATHER
with the Holy Angels.

Mark 9:42–48

"But whoever causes one of these little ones who believe in Me to stumble, it would be better for him if a millstone were hung around his neck, and he were thrown into the sea.

[43] **If your hand causes you to sin, cut it off**. It is better for you to enter into life maimed, **rather than having two hands, to go to hell,** into the fire that shall never be quenched—

[44] **where 'Their worm does not die and the fire is not quenched.'**

[45] And **if your foot causes you to sin, cut it off**. It is better for you to enter life lame, **rather than having two feet, to be cast into hell,** into the fire that shall never be quenched—

[46] **where 'Their worm does not die, and the fire is not quenched.'**

[47] And **if your eye causes you to sin, pluck it out**. It is better for you to enter the kingdom of God with one eye, **rather than having two eyes, to be cast into hell fire—**

[48] **where 'Their worm does not die and the fire is not quenched.'**
(Refers to Is. 66:24)

IF YOUR HAND causes you to sin,

CUT IT OFF ...rather than having 2 HANDS,

to GO to HELL,

... *where* 'Their WORM does NOT DIE &

the *Fire is NOT quenched.*'

IF YOUR FOOT causes you to sin,

CUT IT OFF ...rather than having 2 FEET,

to be CAST into HELL,

... *where* 'Their WORM does NOT DIE, &

the *Fire is NOT quenched.*'

IF YOUR EYE causes you to sin,

PLUCK it OUT ...rather than having 2 EYES,

to be CAST into HELL Fire

- *where* 'Their WORM does NOT DIE &

the *Fire is NOT quenched.*'

Mark 10:2–9

The Pharisees came and asked Him, "Is it lawful for a man to divorce *his* wife?" testing Him.

[3] And **He answered** and said to them, **"What did Moses command** you?"

[4] **They said, "Moses permitted** *a man* **to write a certificate of divorce,** and to dismiss her."

[5] And Jesus answered and said to them, **"Because of the hardness of your heart he wrote you this precept.**

[6] But from the beginning of the creation, God 'made them male and female.'

[7] 'For this reason a man shall leave his father and mother and be joined to his wife,

[8] and the two shall become one flesh';** so then they are no longer two, but one flesh.

[9] **Therefore what God has joined together, let not man separate."**
(Refers to Gen. 1:27, 5:2, 2:24)

The Pharisees came and asked Him,

"Is it lawful for a man to Divorce his wife?"

TESTING HIM.

He answered… "What did Moses command …?"

They said, "Moses permitted a man to write a Certificate of Divorce…"

"Because of the

HARDNESS of your HEART

he wrote you this PRECEPT.

But from the Beginning

of the Creation,

God 'made them

Male & Female. '

'For this reason a man shall leave his father and mother and be joined to his wife, and the two shall become one flesh'…

THEREFORE WHAT GOD HAS JOINED

TOGETHER, LET NOT MAN SEPARATE."

Mark 10:17-21, 29-30

[17] Now as He was going out on the road, one came running, knelt before Him, and asked Him, **"Good Teacher, what shall I do that I may inherit eternal life?"**

[18] So **Jesus said to him,** "Why do you call Me good? No one is good but One, that is, God.

[19] **You know the commandments: 'Do not commit adultery,' 'Do not murder,' 'Do not steal,' 'Do not bear false witness,' 'Do not defraud,' 'Honor your father and your mother.'"**

[20] And he answered and said to Him, "Teacher, all these things I have kept from my youth."
[21] Then Jesus, looking at him, loved him, and said to him, "One thing you lack: Go your way, sell whatever you have and give to the poor, and you will have treasure in heaven; and **come, take up the cross, and follow Me."**

[29] So Jesus answered and said, "Assuredly, I say to you, **there is no one who has left house** or brothers or sisters or father or mother **or wife or children or lands, for My sake and the gospel's,**
[30] **who shall not receive a hundredfold now in this time—** houses and brothers and sisters and mothers and children and lands, **with persecutions—and in the age to come, eternal life.**

"Good Teacher, what shall I do that I may inherit Eternal Life?" So Jesus said to him... "You Know

The Commandments:

'Do not commit adultery,'

'Do not murder,'

'Do not steal,'

'Do not bear false witness,'

'Do not defraud,'

'Honor your father and your mother.'"

Come, take up the cross, & follow Me.

There is NO ONE who has left house... or wife or children or lands,

for My sake and the Gospel's, who shall not receive a $100X$

NOW in this time—

...with persecutions—

and in the AGE TO COME,

Eternal Life.

Mark 11:17

Then He taught, saying to them, *"Is it not written*, **'My house shall be called a house of prayer for all nations'?"** But you have made it a 'den of thieves' (Refers to Is. 56:7, Jer.7:11)

Mark 12:10–11

Have you not even read *this Scripture*: 'The stone which the builders rejected has become the chief cornerstone," [11] This was the LORD's doing, and it is marvelous in our eyes'?" (Refers to Ps. 118:22-23)

Mark 12:24–27

Jesus answered and said to them, **"Are you not therefore mistaken, because you do not know the Scriptures nor the power of God?** [25] For when they rise from the dead, they neither marry nor are given in marriage, but are like angels in heaven. [26] **But concerning the dead,** that they rise, **have you not read in the book of Moses, in the burning bush passage, how God spoke to him, saying, 'I am the God of Abraham, the God of Isaac, and the God of Jacob'?** [27] **He is not the God of the dead, but the God of the living.** You are therefore greatly mistaken." (Refers to Ex.3: 6, 15)

Then He taught, saying to them,

"IS IT NOT WRITTEN,

'My House shall be called a House of Prayer for All Nations'?"

Are you NOT therefore Mistaken, because you DO NOT KNOW the Scriptures nor the POWER of God?

But concerning THE DEAD... have you not read in the Book of Moses, in the BURNING BUSH passage, how God spoke to him, saying,

'I am the God of Abraham, the God of Isaac, and the God of Jacob'?

He is not the God of the DEAD, but the God of the LIVING.

Mark 12:29–31

Jesus answered him, **"The first of all the commandments *is:* 'Hear, O Israel, the LORD our God, the LORD is one.** [30] **And you shall love the LORD your God with all your heart, with all your soul, with all your mind, and with all your strength.' This is the first commandment.** [31] And the second, like *it, is* this: 'You shall love your neighbor as yourself.' There is no other commandment greater than these." (Refers to Deut. 6:4-5, Lev. 19:18)

Mark 12:35–37

Then Jesus answered and said, while He taught in the temple, "How is it that the scribes say that the Christ is the Son of David? [36] For David himself said by the Holy Spirit: 'The LORD said to my Lord, "Sit at My right hand, till I make Your enemies Your footstool."' [37] Therefore David himself calls Him 'Lord'; how is He *then* his Son?" And the common people heard Him gladly. (Refers to Ps. 110:1)

THE 1ST OF ALL

the COMMANDMENTS is:

'Hear, O Israel,

THE LORD OUR GOD,

The LORD is

One.

And you shall Love

the LORD your God

with all your Heart,

with all your Soul,

with all your Mind,

and with all your Strength.'

This is the FIRST COMMANDMENT.

Mark 13:3–4, 10, 14

Now as He sat on the Mount of Olives opposite the temple, Peter, James, John, and Andrew asked Him privately,

⁴ **"Tell us, when will these things be?** And what *will be* the sign when all these things will be fulfilled?"

¹⁰ And **the gospel must first be preached to all the nations.**

¹⁴ "So when you see the 'abomination of desolation,' spoken of by Daniel the prophet, standing where it ought not" (let the reader understand), "then let those who are in Judea flee to the mountains.
(Refers to Dan. 11:31, 12:11)

Mark 13:31

Heaven and earth will pass away, but *My words* will by no means pass away.

Mark 14:21

The Son of Man indeed goes just as it is written of Him, but woe to that man by whom the Son of Man is betrayed! It would have been good for that man if he had never been born."

Tell us, when will these things be?

The Gospel MUST FIRST BE PREACHED TO ALL THE NATIONS.

Heaven and Earth WILL PASS AWAY, BUT MY WORDS *will By No Means pass away.*

The Son of Man indeed goes just as it is written of Him, but WOE to that MAN by whom the Son of Man is betrayed! It would have been Good FOR THAT MAN if he had never been born.

Mark 14:27

Then Jesus said to them, **"All of you will be made to stumble because of Me this night, for** *it is written*: **'I will strike the Shepherd, and the sheep will be scattered."**
(Refers to Zech. 13:7)

Mark 14:46–49

Then they laid their hands on Him and took Him. [47] And one of those who stood by drew his sword and struck the servant of the high priest, and cut off his ear. [48] Then Jesus answered and said to them, "Have you come out, as against a robber, with swords and clubs to take Me? [49] **I was daily with you in the temple teaching, and you did not seize Me. But the Scriptures must be fulfilled."**

Mark 15:34

And at the ninth hour Jesus cried out with a loud voice, saying, "Eloi, Eloi, lama sabachthani?" which is translated, "My God, My God, why have You forsaken Me?" (Refers to Ps. 22:1)

Mark 16:15

And He said to them, **"Go into all the world and preach the** *gospel* **to every creature."**

ALL OF YOU WILL BE MADE TO STUMBLE because of Me this night, *for it is written:* 'I WILL STRIKE THE SHEPHERD, AND THE SHEEP WILL BE SCATTERED.' *I was Daily with you in the Temple teaching,* AND YOU DID NOT SEIZE ME. *But the Scriptures Must Be Fulfilled.* GO INTO ALL THE WORLD & Preach The Gospel *to Every Creature.*

Luke

Luke 4:1–4

Then **Jesus**, being filled with the Holy Spirit, returned from the Jordan and was led by the Spirit into the wilderness,
[2] being **tempted for forty days by the devil**. And in those days He ate nothing, and afterward, when they had ended, He was hungry.
[3] And the devil said to Him, "If You are the Son of God, command this stone to become bread."
[4] But Jesus answered him, saying, *"It is written*, **'Man shall not live by bread alone, but by every word of God.'"**
(Refers to Deut. 8:3)

Luke 4:8–12

And Jesus answered and said to him, **"Get behind Me, Satan! For it is written, 'You shall worship the LORD your God, and Him only you shall serve.'"**
[9] Then he brought Him to Jerusalem, set Him on the pinnacle of the temple, and said to Him, "If You are the Son of God, throw Yourself down from here.
[10] For it is written: 'He shall give His angels charge over you, to keep you,'
[11] and, 'In *their* hands they shall bear you up, lest you dash your foot against a stone.'"
[12] And Jesus answered and said to him, **"It has been said, 'You shall not tempt the LORD your God.'"**
(Refers to Deut. 6:13, Ps. 91:11-12, Deut. 6:16)

It is written,

'Man shall not Live by Bread alone, but by EVERY Word of God.'

GET BEHIND ME, SATAN!

For it is written,

'YOU SHALL WORSHIP THE LORD YOUR GOD, & HIM ONLY YOU SHALL SERVE.'

'You shall not Tempt the LORD your God.'

Luke 4:16–21

And as His custom was, He (Jesus) went into the synagogue on the Sabbath day, and stood up to read.

17 And He was handed the book of the prophet Isaiah. And when He had opened the book, He found the place where it was written:

18 "The Spirit of the LORD *is* upon me, because He has anointed me to preach the gospel to *the* poor; He has sent me to heal the brokenhearted, to proclaim liberty to *the captives* and recovery of sight to *the* blind, *to* set at liberty those who are oppressed;

19 to proclaim the acceptable year of the LORD."

20 Then He closed the book, and gave *it* back to the attendant and sat down. And the eyes of all who were in the synagogue were fixed on Him.

21 And He began to say to them, "Today this Scripture is fulfilled in your hearing."

And as His custom was, He (Jesus) went into the synagogue on the Sabbath day, and stood up to read.

"The Spirit of the LORD

is upon Me,

because He has Anointed Me

to PREACH THE GOSPEL to the Poor;

HE HAS SENT ME TO HEAL

THE BROKENHEARTED,

to Proclaim Liberty

to the Captives

& Recovery of Sight

to the Blind,

to set at Liberty

those who are Oppressed...

Today this Scripture is

FULFILLED in your hearing."

Luke 4:24-27

Then He said, "**Assuredly, I say to you, no prophet is accepted in his own country.**

25 **But I tell you truly, many widows were in Israel in the days of Elijah,** when the heaven was shut up three years and six months, **and there was a great famine** throughout all the land;

26 but **to none of them was Elijah sent except to Zarephath,** *in the region* of Sidon, to a woman who was **a widow.**
(Refers to I Kings 17:9)

27 And **many lepers were in Israel in the time of Elisha** the prophet, and **none of them was cleansed except Naaman the Syrian.**"
(Refers to II Kings 5:1-14)

Luke 5:14

And He charged him to tell no one, "But go and show yourself to the priest, and make an offering for your cleansing, as a testimony to them, just as Moses commanded."

Assuredly, I say to you,

NO PROPHET

Is Accepted

in his Own Country.

But I tell you truly,

Many Widows were in Israel in the

Days *of* Elijah...

and there was a Great Famine...

TO NONE of them was Elijah sent
EXCEPT to Zarephath, to a widow.

MANY Lepers were in Israel in the

Time *of* Elisha...

NONE of them was CLEANSED
EXCEPT Naaman the Syrian.

Luke 6:2–5

And some of **the Pharisees said** to them, **"Why are you doing what is not lawful to do on the Sabbath?"**
[3] **But Jesus** answering them **said, "Have you not even read this, what David did** when he was hungry, he and those who were with him:
[4] **how he went into the house of God, took and ate the showbread,** and also gave some to those with him, **which is not lawful for any but the priests to eat?"**
[5] And He said to them, **"The Son of Man is also Lord of the Sabbath."**

Luke 6:8–10

But He knew their thoughts, and said to the man who had the withered hand, "Arise and stand here." And he arose and stood.
[9] Then Jesus said to them, **"I will ask you one thing: Is it lawful on the Sabbath to do good or to do evil, to save life or to destroy?"**
[10] And when He had looked around at them all, He said to the man, "Stretch out your hand." And he did so, and his hand was restored as whole as the other.

...the Pharisees said...

"WHY are you doing what is NOT Lawful to do on the Sabbath?"

But Jesus ...said,

"Have you not even read this, what David did ... how he went into the House of God, TOOK & ATE the Showbread... WHICH IS NOT LAWFUL for any but the Priests to eat?"

"The Son of Man is also Lord of the Sabbath."

"I WILL ASK YOU ONE THING: Is it lawful on the Sabbath to do Good or to do Evil, to Save life or to Destroy?"

Luke 6:46–49

"But why do you call Me 'Lord, Lord,' and not do the things which I say?

47 **Whoever** comes to Me, and **hears My sayings and does them**, I will show you whom he is like:

48 He **is like a man building a house, who** dug deep and laid the foundation on the rock.

And when the flood arose, the stream beat vehemently **against that house, and could not shake it, for it was founded on the rock.**

49 But he who heard and did nothing

is like a man who built a house on the earth without a foundation,

against which the stream beat vehemently;

and immediately it fell.

And the ruin of that house was great."

Luke 7:27

This is he of whom *it is written*:

'Behold, I send My messenger before Your face, who will prepare Your way before You.'
(Refers to Mal.3:1)

Why do you call Me 'Lord, Lord',

& NOT DO the things which I say?

Whoever... hears My sayings

& DOES THEM,

...is like a man building a house,

WHO... LAID THE FOUNDATION

ON THE ROCK.

And when the flood arose,

THE STREAM BEAT... AGAINST THAT HOUSE,

& Could Not Shake It,

FOR IT WAS FOUNDED

ON THE ROCK!

But he who heard & DID NOTHING

is like a man who built a house on the earth

WITHOUT A FOUNDATION,

...and immediately it FELL.

And the RUIN of that house WAS GREAT!

Luke 8:10–15

And He said, "To you it has been given to know the mysteries of the kingdom of God, but to the rest *it is given in parables*, that 'Seeing they may not see, and hearing they may not understand.'

[11] **"Now the parable is this: The seed is the *word of God**. [12] Those by the wayside are the ones who hear; then the devil comes and takes away *the word* out of their hearts, lest they should believe and be saved.**

[13] But the ones on the rock *are those* who, when they hear, receive **the word** with joy; and these have no root, who believe for a while and in time of temptation fall away.

[14] **Now the ones *that* fell among thorns are those who, when they have heard (*the word*), go out and are choked with cares, riches, and pleasures of life, and bring no fruit to maturity.**

[15] **But the ones that fell on the good ground are those who, having heard the word with a noble and good heart, keep it and bear fruit with patience.** (Refers to Is. 6:9)

NOW THE PARABLE IS THIS:

THE SEED IS THE WORD OF GOD...

Then the devil comes and takes away

THE WORD *out of their hearts,*

lest they should believe and be SAVED...

Now the ones that fell among thorns

are those who, when they have heard (the word),

go out and ARE CHOKED WITH

CARES,

RICHES,

& PLEASURES of life,

& bring NO FRUIT to maturity.

But the ones that fell on the GOOD GROUND

are those who, having HEARD *the Word with a*

NOBLE & GOOD HEART,

KEEP IT

& BEAR FRUIT *with patience.*

Luke 8:21

But He answered and said to them, **"My mother and My brothers are these who hear the** *word* **of God and do it."**

Luke 9:26

For whoever is ashamed of Me and *My words*, **of him the Son of Man will be ashamed when He comes in His** *own* **glory, and** *in His* **Father's, and of the holy angel.**

Luke 10:25–28

And behold, **a certain lawyer stood up and tested Him**, saying, "Teacher, what shall I do to inherit eternal life?"

[26] He said to him, **"What is written in the law?** What is your reading *of it?"*

[27] So he answered and said, **"You shall love the LORD your God with all your heart, with all your soul, with all your strength, and with all your mind, and your neighbor as yourself."**

[28] And He said to him, **"You have answered rightly; do this and you will live."** (Refers to Deut. 6:5, Lev. 19:18)

My Mother & My Brothers are those Who HEAR the Word of God and DO IT.

For whoever is Ashamed of Me & My Words, of him the Son of Man will be ASHAMED when He comes in His OWN GLORY, & in His Father's, & of the Holy Angel.

…a certain LAWYER stood up and TESTED Him…

(Jesus said to him) "What is WRITTEN in THE LAW?"

"You shall LOVE the LORD your God with all your HEART, with all your SOUL, with all your STRENGTH, and with all your MIND, and 'your neighbor as yourself."

"You have answered rightly; do this and you will LIVE."

Luke 10:38–42

Now it happened as they went that He entered a certain village; and a certain woman named **Martha welcomed Him into her house.**

[39] **And she had a sister called Mary, who also** *sat at Jesus' feet and heard His word.*

[40] **But Martha was distracted with much serving,** and she approached Him and said, "Lord, do You not care that my sister has left me to serve alone? Therefore tell her to help me."

[41] And Jesus answered and said to her, **"Martha, Martha, you are worried and troubled about many things.**

[42] **But one thing is needed, and Mary has chosen that good part, which will not be taken away from her."**

Martha WELCOMED HIM into her house. And she had a sister CALLED *Mary,* WHO ALSO SAT AT JESUS' FEET AND HEARD HIS WORD. BUT MARTHA WAS *distracted* WITH MUCH SERVING... *Martha, Martha,* YOU ARE **worried & troubled** ABOUT MANY THINGS. But ONE THING is needed, *& Mary has chosen that Good Part,* WHICH WILL NOT BE TAKEN AWAY FROM HER."

Luke 11:27–32

And it happened, as He spoke these things, that a certain woman from the crowd raised her voice and said to Him, "Blessed *is* the womb that bore You, and *the* breasts which nursed You!"

28 But He said, "More than that, **blessed are those who hear the word of God and keep it!"**

29 And while the crowds were thickly gathered together, He began to say, "This is an evil generation. It seeks a sign, and no sign will be given to it except the sign of Jonah the prophet.

30 **For as Jonah became a sign to the Ninevites, so also the Son of Man will be to this generation.**

31 **The queen of the South will rise up in the judgment with the men of this generation** and condemn them, for she came from the ends of the earth to hear the wisdom of Solomon; and indeed **a greater than Solomon** *is* **here.**

32 **The men of Nineveh will rise up in the judgment with this generation and condemn it**, for they repented at the preaching of Jonah; and indeed **a greater than Jonah** *is* here.

Luke 13:35

See! Your house is left to you desolate; and assuredly, I say to you, **you shall not see Me until** *the time* **comes when you say, 'Blessed is He who comes in the name of the Lord!'**
(Refers to Ps. 118:26)

...blessed are those WHO

HEAR the Word of God

and KEEP IT!

For as Jonah became

A SIGN TO THE NINEVITES,

so also the Son of Man

WILL BE TO THIS GENERATION.

The Queen of the South will rise up

in the Judgment with the men of this Generation...

A GREATER

THAN SOLOMON IS HERE.

The men of Nineveh will rise up

in the Judgment with this Generation and Condemn It...

INDEED A GREATER

THAN JONAH IS HERE.

...you shall not see Me until the time comes when you say,

'Blessed is He who comes in the name of the LORD!'

Luke 16:16–17

The law and the prophets were until John. Since that time the kingdom of God has been preached, and everyone is pressing into it. [17] **And it is easier for heaven and earth to pass away than for one tittle** *of the law* **to fail.**

Luke 16:31

But he said to him, **"If they do not hear Moses and the prophets, neither will they be persuaded though one rise from the dead."**

Luke 17:26–32

And as it was in the days of Noah, so it will be also in the days of the Son of Man: [27] They ate, they drank, they married wives, they were given in marriage, until the day that Noah entered the ark, and the flood came and destroyed them all. [28] **Likewise as it was also in the days of Lot**: They ate, they drank, they bought, they sold, they planted, they built; [29] but on the day that Lot went out of Sodom it rained fire and brimstone from heaven and destroyed *them* all. [30] **Even so will it be in the day when the Son of Man is revealed.** [31] "In that day, he who is on the housetop, and his goods are in the house, let him not come down to take them away. And likewise the one who is in the field, let him not turn back. [32] Remember Lot's wife.

The Law and the Prophets were until John.

And it is easier for Heaven & Earth

to Pass Away than

for one tittle of the Law to fail.

If they DO NOT HEAR

MOSES & the Prophets,

NEITHER WILL THEY

be persuaded though one

RISE FROM THE DEAD.

And as it was in the **Days of Noah,** so it will be also in the

Days of the Son of Man...

Likewise as it was also in the **Days of Lot...**

Even so will it be in the Day when

the Son of Man IS REVEALED.

Luke 18:20

"You know *the commandments*: 'Do not commit adultery,' 'Do not murder,' 'Do not steal,' 'Do not bear false witness,' 'Honor your father and your mother.'"
(Refers to Ex. 20:12-16, Deut. 5:16-20)

Luke 18:31

Then He took the twelve aside and said to them, **"Behold, we are going up to Jerusalem, and all things that are written by the prophets concerning the Son of Man will be accomplished.**

Luke 19:45–46

Then He went into the temple and began to drive out those who bought and sold in it [46] saying to them, **"It is written, 'My house is a house of prayer**,' but you have made it a 'den of thieves.'"
(Refers to Is. 56:7, Jer. 7:11)

Luke 20:17

Then He looked at them and said, "What then is this **that** *is written*: 'The stone which the builders rejected has become the chief cornerstone'?
(Refers to Ps. 118:22)

Behold,

we are going up to

JERUSALEM,

And all things that are

Written

by the

Prophets

concerning the Son of Man

will be Accomplished.

It is written,

'MY HOUSE IS A

HOUSE OF

PRAYER,'…

Luke 20:37–38

But even Moses showed in the *burning* **bush** *passage* **that the dead are raised, when he called the Lord 'the God of Abraham, the God of Isaac, and the God of Jacob.'**

[38] **For He is not the God of the dead but of the living, for all live to Him. (Refers to Ex. 3:6-7)**

Luke 20:41–44

Then Jesus said to them, "Why is it said that the Messiah is the son of David?
[42] Now David himself said in the Book of Psalms: 'The LORD said to my Lord, "Sit at My right hand,

[43] Till I make Your enemies Your footstool."'

[44] Therefore David calls Him 'Lord'; how is He then his Son?"
(Refers to Ps. 110:1)

Luke 21:22

[22] **For these are the days of vengeance, that all things which are written may be fulfilled.**

Luke 21:33

Heaven and earth will pass away, but *My* words will by no means pass away.

But even Moses showed in the

Burning Bush passage

that the DEAD are raised,

WHEN he called the Lord

'the God of Abraham,

the God of Isaac,

and the God of Jacob.'

For He is not the

God of the dead

but of the Living,

FOR ALL *Live to Him.*

For these are the

Days of Vengeance

that all things which are written may be FULFILLED.

Heaven & Earth WILL PASS AWAY,

but MY WORDS

will **by no means** pass away.

Luke 22:37

For I say to you that this which is written must still be accomplished in Me: 'And He was numbered with the transgressors.' For the things concerning Me have an end.
(Refers to Is. 53:12)

Luke 23:46

And when Jesus had cried out with a loud voice, He said, **"Father, 'into Your hands I commit My spirit.'"** Having said this, He breathed His last.
(Refers to Ps. 31:5)

Luke 24:27

And beginning at Moses and all the Prophets, He expounded to them in all the Scriptures the things concerning Himself.

Luke 24:44

Then He said to them, **"These *are* the words which I spoke to you while I was still with you, that all things must be fulfilled which were written in the Law of Moses and the Prophets and *the* Psalms concerning Me."**

Luke 24:46

Then He said to them, **"Thus *it is written*, and thus it was necessary for the Christ to suffer and to rise from the dead the third day."**

For I say to you that this <u>which is Written</u> *must* still be accomplished in Me:

'And He was numbered with the **transgressors.**'

FOR THE THINGS CONCERNING ME HAVE **AN END.**

"Father, 'into Your hands I commit My Spirit.'"

THESE ARE THE WORDS which I SPOKE TO YOU while I was STILL WITH YOU that all things MUST BE FULFILLED which were *WRITTEN IN*

The Law of Moses &

The Prophets &

The Psalms

concerning Me.

Thus it is Written, & THUS it was NECESSARY

FOR THE CHRIST TO SUFFER & TO RISE FROM THE DEAD THE 3RD DAY.

 John

John 1:1–4

In the beginning was *the Word*, and the Word was with God, and *the Word was God*.

[2] He was in the beginning with God.

[3] All things were made *through Him*, and *without Him* nothing was made that was made.

[4] *In Him* was life, and the life was the light of men.

John 1:14

And *the Word* became flesh and dwelt among us, and we beheld His glory, the glory as of the only begotten of the Father, full of grace and truth.

In the Beginning WAS *The Word...*

THE WORD

WAS WITH GOD...

The Word was God.

And the Word

Became Flesh

& Dwelt Among Us,

& WE BEHELD HIS GLORY,

the Glory

AS OF THE ONLY BEGOTTEN OF THE FATHER,

Full of Grace & Truth.

John 5:24–26

"Most assuredly, I say to you, **he who hears My *word* and believes in Him who sent Me has everlasting life, and shall not come into judgment, but has passed from death into life.**

[25] Most assuredly, I say to you, **the hour is coming, and now is, when the dead will hear the voice of the Son of God; and those who hear will live.**

[26] For as the Father has life in Himself, so He has granted the Son to have life in Himself.

John 5:38–39

But you do not have His word abiding in you, because whom He sent, Him you do not believe.

[39] You search *the Scriptures*, for in them you think you have eternal life; and these are they which testify of Me.

HE WHO HEARS *My Word* & *Believes* IN HIM WHO SENT ME HAS EVERLASTING LIFE, AND *Shall Not* COME INTO JUDGMENT, BUT HAS PASSED FROM *Death into Life.* *The Hour* is coming, and NOW IS, when the DEAD will HEAR *the Voice of the Son of God:* & those who HEAR will LIVE.

But you do not have His Word ABIDING in you, BECAUSE whom He sent, Him YOU DO NO BELIEVE!

John 5:45–47

Do not think that I shall accuse you to the Father; **there is** *one* **who accuses you—Moses, in whom you trust.**

[46] **For if you believed Moses, you would believe Me; for he wrote about Me.**

[47] **But if you do not believe his writings, how will you believe My words?"**

John 6:45

It is written **in the prophets, 'And they shall all be taught by God.' Therefore everyone who has heard and learned from the Father comes to Me.**

(Refers to Is. 54:13)

...there's ONE who ACCUSES you—MOSES, *in whom you* TRUST.

For if you BELIEVED Moses,

you would BELIEVE Me;

for he wrote about Me.

But IF you DO NOT BELIEVE his writings,

HOW will you BELIEVE My Words?

It is Written

in the Prophets,

'And they shall ALL be taught by God.'

Therefore

EVERYONE WHO HAS

HEARD & LEARNED

FROM THE FATHER

COMES TO ME.

John 6:63

It is the Spirit who gives life; the flesh profits nothing. *The words* that I speak to you are spirit, and they are life.

John 7:16–19

Jesus answered them and said, **"My doctrine is not Mine, but His who sent Me.**

[17] **If anyone wills to do His will, he shall know concerning** *the doctrine*, **whether it is from God or whether I speak on My own authority.**

[18] He who speaks from himself seeks his own glory; but He who seeks the glory of the One who sent Him is true, and no unrighteousness is in Him.

[19] Did not Moses give you the law, yet none of you keeps the law? Why do you seek to kill Me?"

It is the Spirit
Who gives Life;
THE FLESH PROFITS NOTHING.
The Words
that I speak to you
ARE Spirit,
and they ARE Life.
MY DOCTRINE IS NOT
MINE, BUT HIS WHO SENT ME.
IF anyone WILLS
to do HIS WILL,
HE SHALL KNOW CONCERNING
THE DOCTRINE,
whether it is from God
or whether I speak on My own authority.

John 7:23–24

If a man receives circumcision on the Sabbath, so that the law of Moses should not be broken, are you angry with Me because I made a man completely well on the Sabbath?

24 Do not judge according to appearance, but judge with righteous judgment."

John 7:38

He who believes in Me, as *the Scripture* has said, out of his heart will flow rivers of living water."

John 8:17

It is also *written in your law* that the testimony of two men is true.

John 8:31–32

Then Jesus said to those Jews who believed Him, **"If you abide in *My word*, you are My disciples indeed.**

32 **And you shall know the truth, and the truth shall make you free."**

He who Believes in Me,

as the Scripture has said,

out of his Heart

will flow Rivers

of Living Water.

It is also Written in your Law that

the Testimony of two men is true.

If you ABIDE in MY WORD,

you ARE My Disciples INDEED.

And you shall

KNOW the TRUTH,

& The TRUTH

shall make you FREE.

JOANN JERNIGAN

John 8:37

"I know that you are Abraham's descendants, but you seek to kill Me, because My word has no place in you.

John 8:43

Why do you not understand My speech? Because you are not able to listen to My word.

John 8:47

He who is of God hears God's words; therefore you do not hear, because you are not of God."

John 8:51

Most assuredly, I say to you, if anyone keeps My word he shall never see death."

John 8:55

Yet you have not known Him, but I know Him. And if I say, 'I do not know Him,' I shall be a liar like you; but I do know Him, and keep His word

I know that you are Abraham's descendants, but you seek to KILL ME, BECAUSE My Word has NO PLACE IN YOU. …YOU ARE NOT ABLE TO LISTEN TO MY WORD. He who is OF God HEARS God's Words; therefore YOU DO NOT HEAR, because YOU ARE NOT OF GOD. Most assuredly, I say to you, IF ANYONE Keeps My Word he shall NEVER SEE Death. And if I say, 'I do not know Him,' I shall be A LIAR like you; but I do Know Him, and KEEP His Word.

52

John 10:17–18

"Therefore My Father loves Me, because I lay down My life that I may take it again.

[18] No one takes it from Me, but I lay it down of Myself. **I have power to lay it down, and I have power to take it again. This command I have received from My Father."**

John 10:34–36

Jesus answered them, "Is it not written in your law, 'I said, "You are gods"'?

[35] If He called them gods, to whom the word of God came **(and the Scripture cannot be broken),**

[36] do you say of Him whom the Father sanctified and sent into the world, 'You are blaspheming,' because I said, 'I am the Son of God'? (Refers to Ps. 82:6)

Therefore My Father loves Me, BECAUSE I LAY DOWN My Life THAT I may TAKE IT AGAIN. I HAVE POWER TO LAY IT DOWN, AND I HAVE POWER TO TAKE IT AGAIN. This Command I have received from My Father. (and the Scripture cannot be broken)

John 12:47–50

And if anyone hears My words and does not believe, I do not judge him; for I did not come to judge the world but to save the world.

[48] He who rejects Me, and does not receive My words, has that which judges him—the word that I have spoken will judge him in the last day.

[49] For I have not spoken on My own authority; but the Father who sent Me gave Me a command, what I should say and what I should speak.

[50] And I know that His command is everlasting life. Therefore, whatever I speak, just as the Father has told Me, so I speak."

AND IF ANYONE HEARS

My Words

& DOES NOT BELIEVE,

I DO NOT JUDGE him;

for I did not come to JUDGE the WORLD,

but to SAVE the WORLD.

He who REJECTS ME, &

DOES NOT RECEIVE My Words,

HAS THAT WHICH JUDGES HIM-

The WORD THAT I HAVE

SPOKEN WILL JUDGE HIM

in the Last Day.

And I know that His Command

Is Everlasting Life.

Therefore, WHATEVER I SPEAK,

just as the FATHER has told Me, SO I SPEAK.

John 13:18

"I do not speak concerning all of you. I know whom I have chosen; but that **the Scripture** may be fulfilled, 'He who eats bread with Me has lifted up his heel against Me.' (Refers to Ps. 41:9)

John 13:34

A new *commandment* I give to you, that you love one another; as I have loved you, that you also love one another.

John 14:15

"If you love Me, keep My commandments.

John 14:21

He who has My commandments and keeps them, it is he who loves Me. And he who loves Me will be loved by My Father, **and I will love him and manifest Myself to him."**

A New Commandment I GIVE TO YOU, THAT YOU Love One Another; AS I HAVE LOVED YOU, that you also LOVE one another.

IF YOU Love Me, KEEP MY COMMANDMENTS.

He who has My Commandments & KEEPS THEM, IT IS HE WHO Loves Me.

...AND I WILL Love HIM & Manifest Myself to him.

John 14:23–24

Jesus answered and said to him, **"If anyone loves Me, he will keep *My word*; and My Father will love him, and We will come to him and make Our home with him.**

[24] **He who does not love Me does not keep *My words*;** and the word which you hear is not Mine but the Father's who sent Me."

John 14:31

But that the world may know that I love the Father, and as the Father gave Me *commandment*, so I do. Arise, let us go from here.

John 15:3

You are already clean because of *the word* which I have spoken to you.

If anyone Loves Me, HE WILL KEEP MY WORD; & My Father will Love him, & WE WILL COME TO HIM & make Our Home with him. He who *DOES NOT LOVE* Me *DOES NOT KEEP* My Words...

But that the world may know that I LOVE THE FATHER, & as the Father gave Me Commandment, so I DO.

You are already CLEAN because of THE WORD WHICH I HAVE spoken to you.

John 15:7

If you abide in Me, and *My words* abide in you, you will ask what you desire, and it shall be done for you.

John 15:10

If you keep *My commandments*, you will abide in My love, just as I have kept *My Father's commandments* and abide in His love.

John 15:12

This is *My commandment*, that you love one another as I have loved you.

If you Abide in Me,
& My Words Abide in you,

you will ASK what you DESIRE,

& IT SHALL BE DONE FOR YOU.

If you

Keep My Commandments

you will Abide

in My Love,

just as I have Kept

My Father's Commandments &

Abide in His Love.

This is My Commandment,

that you Love One Another

as I have loved you.

John 15:20

Remember *the word* that I said to you, 'A servant is not greater than his **master.'** If they persecuted Me, they will also persecute you. If they kept **My word**, they will keep yours also.

John 15:25

But this happened that the word might be fulfilled which is written in their law, 'They hated Me without a cause.'
(Refers to Ps. 69:4)

John 17:6

"I have manifested Your name to the men whom You have given Me out of the world. They were Yours, You gave them to Me, and they have kept your Word.

John 17:8

For I have given to them the words which You have given Me; and they have received them, and have known surely that I came forth from You; and they have believed that You sent Me.

Remember the Word that I said to you, 'A Servant is

Not Greater than his Master.'

But this happened that

THE WORD MIGHT BE FULFILLED

which is Written in their Law,

'THEY HATED ME without a Cause.'

I HAVE MANIFESTED Your Name

to the men whom

You have Given Me

OUT OF THE WORLD.

They were Yours,

You gave them to Me,

& they have Kept Your Word.

For I have GIVEN to them

The Words

which You have GIVEN Me;

& they have RECEIVED THEM . . .

John 17:14

I have given them *Your word*; and the world has hated them because they are not of the world, just as I am not of the world.

John 17:17

Sanctify them by Your truth. Your word is truth.

John 17:19

And for their sakes I sanctify Myself, that they also may be *sanctified by the truth*.

John 18:37

Pilate therefore said to Him, "Are You a king then?" Jesus answered, "You say rightly that I am a king. **For this cause I was born, and for this cause I have come into the world, that I should bear witness to the truth. Everyone who is of the truth hears My voice."**

I have Given them Your Word;

and the World has Hated Them

Because they Are Not of the World,

just as I Am Not of the World.

Sanctify them by Your Truth. Your Word is Truth.

And for their sakes *I Sanctify Myself,*

that they also may be *Sanctified by the Truth.*

FOR THIS CAUSE I WAS BORN,

& For This Cause I have Come into the World,

THAT I SHOULD

BEAR WITNESS TO THE TRUTH.

Everyone Who is of The Truth

Hears My Voice!

The End

About the Author

Though raised a Catholic in an Italian-American family, the author did not have a saving and personal relationship with the Savior and she had never read the BIBLE. Rebellion set in in her teen years and on into adulthood. "Anxiety in the heart of man causes depression, but a good word makes it glad", Proverbs 12:25. At the age of thirty, she cried out to God, not knowing if He even existed.

"For whoever calls on the name of the Lord shall be saved", Romans 10:13. It was a Damascus Road experience, likened to a bolt of lightning and coming face to face with the Living God. As that changed the Apostle Paul completely and forever, so it did the author, exposing and delivering her from a multitude of sins to walk with Christ.

Eventually widowed, she went on as a young single parent to teach for 17 years in Christian schools, serve on several mission trips, and in prison/jail ministry until present day. Her passion has always been for Jesus and His Word, to conform her life and heart to it as empowered by the Holy Spirit, and teaching others to do the same.

Jesus said, "If you love Me, keep My commandments" and "He who does not love Me does not keep my words…" in John 14:15 and 14:23. Jesus IS the Word made flesh, in John 1:14. His name is called the Word of God, from Revelation 19:13.

GO YE in to ALL the world and preach the Gospel. Make disciples of every nation, teaching them everything I have taught you. This is Jesus' Great Commission given in Mark 16:15 and Matthew 28:19-20.

Love the Word. Love Jesus. Follow Jesus. Make disciples.

CPSIA information can be obtained
at www.ICGtesting.com
Printed in the USA
JSHW021235071120
9396JS00003B/34

9 781642 588217